Mom, Where's My Dad?

RATHSI
PUBLISHING

476 Greyhawk Way, Fairburn, GA 30213
(404) 207-0544
www.RATHSIPUBLISHING.com
INFO@RATHSIPUBLISHING.COM

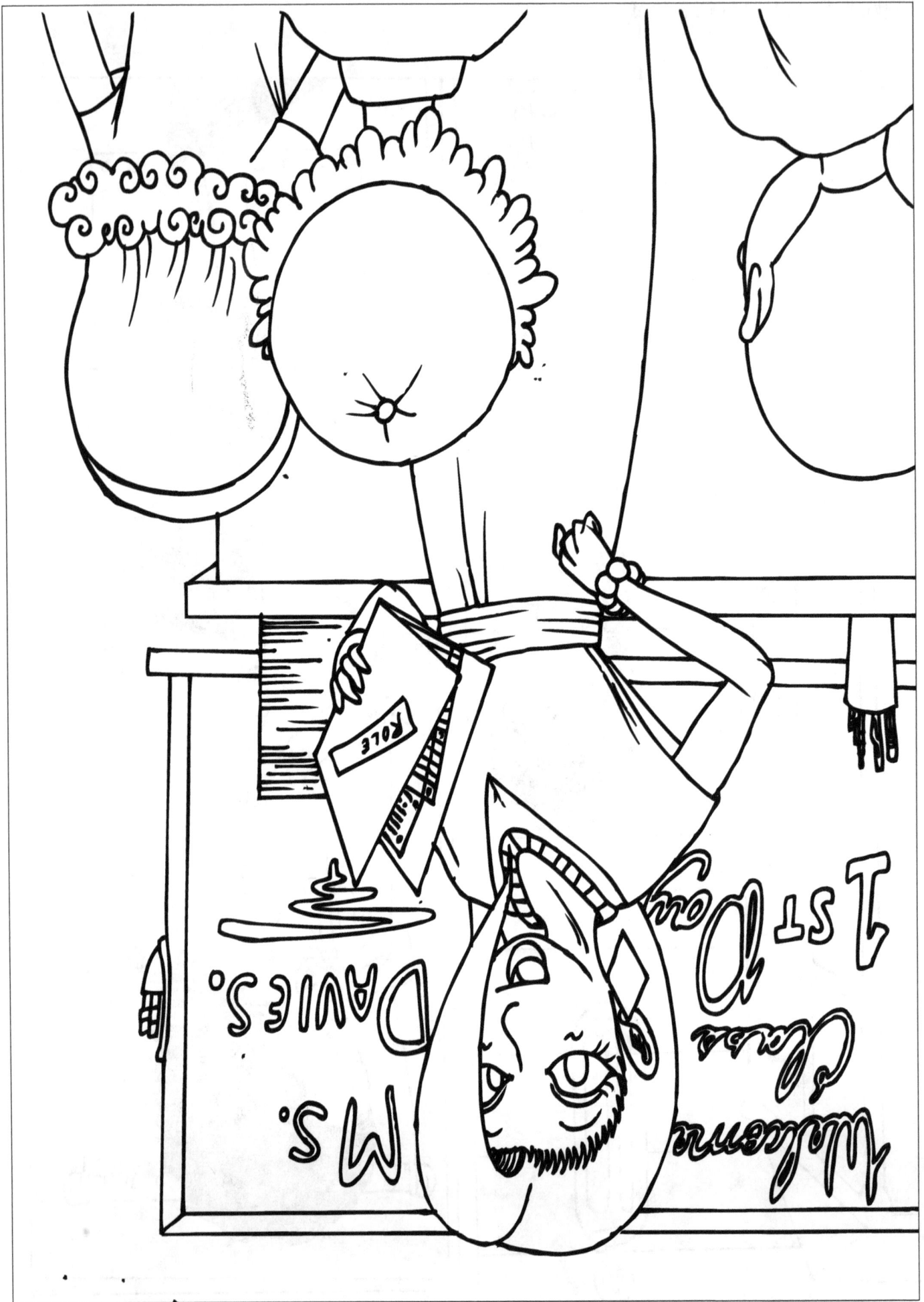

Welcome Class of
Ms. Davies.
1st Day

ROLE

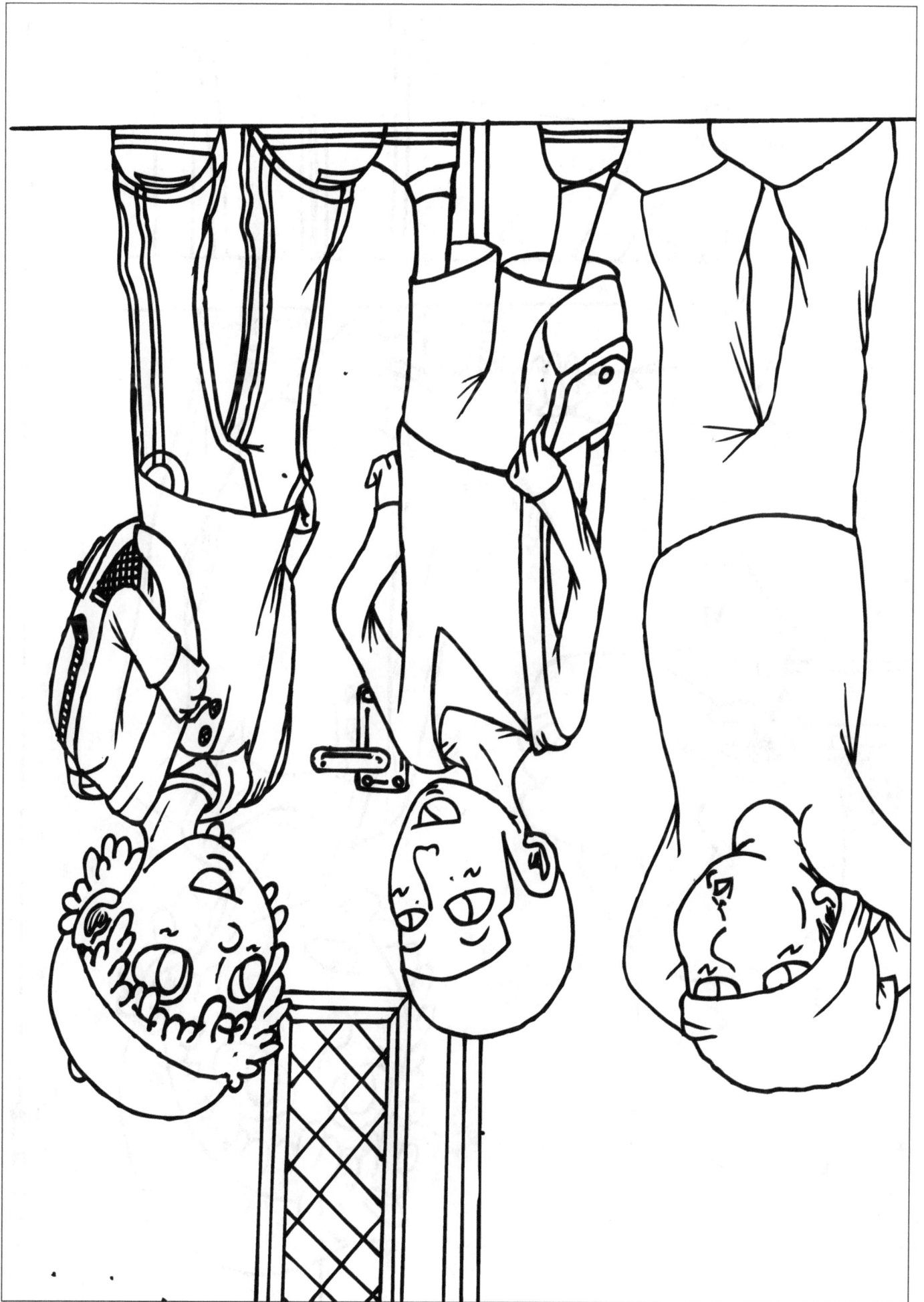

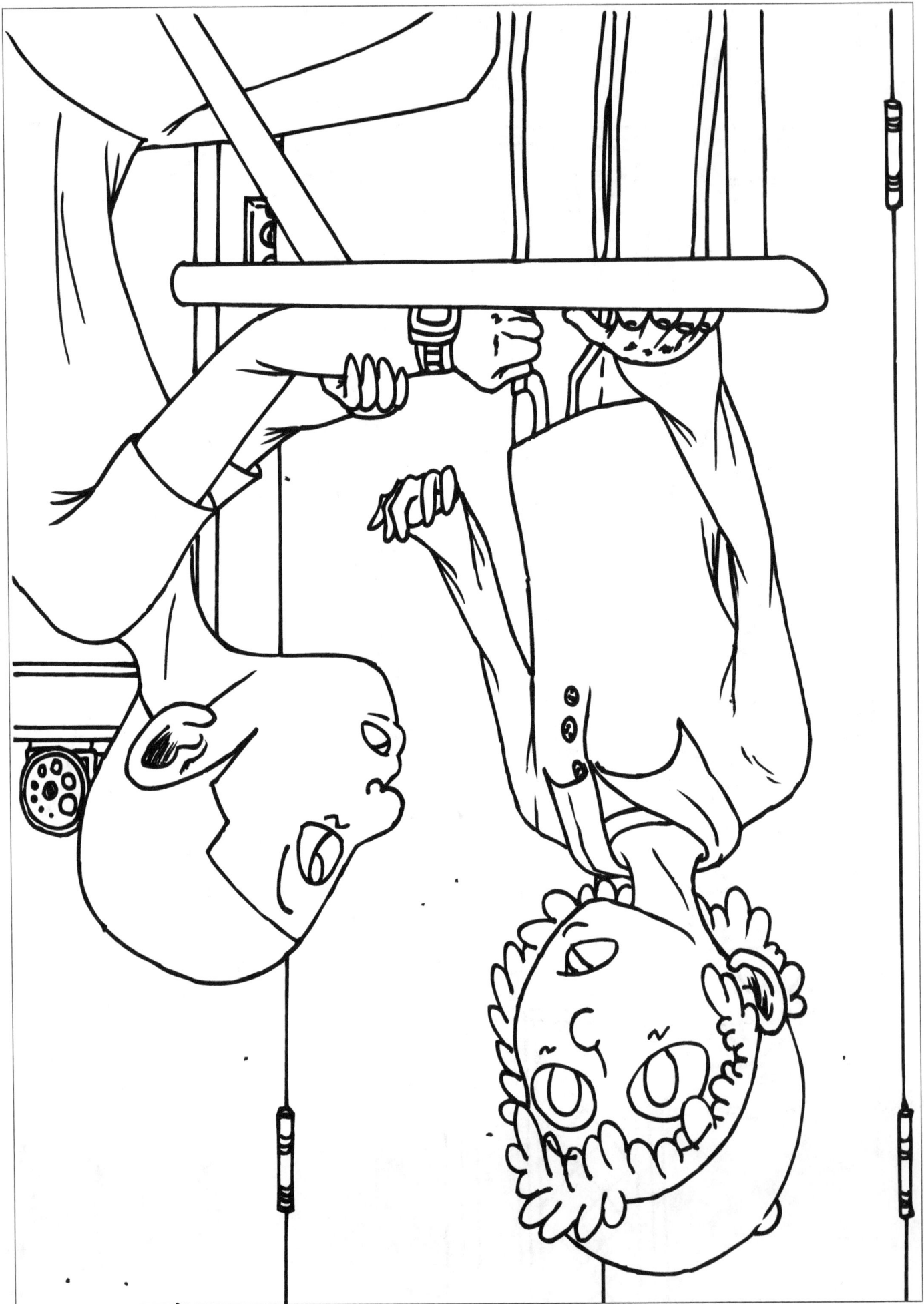

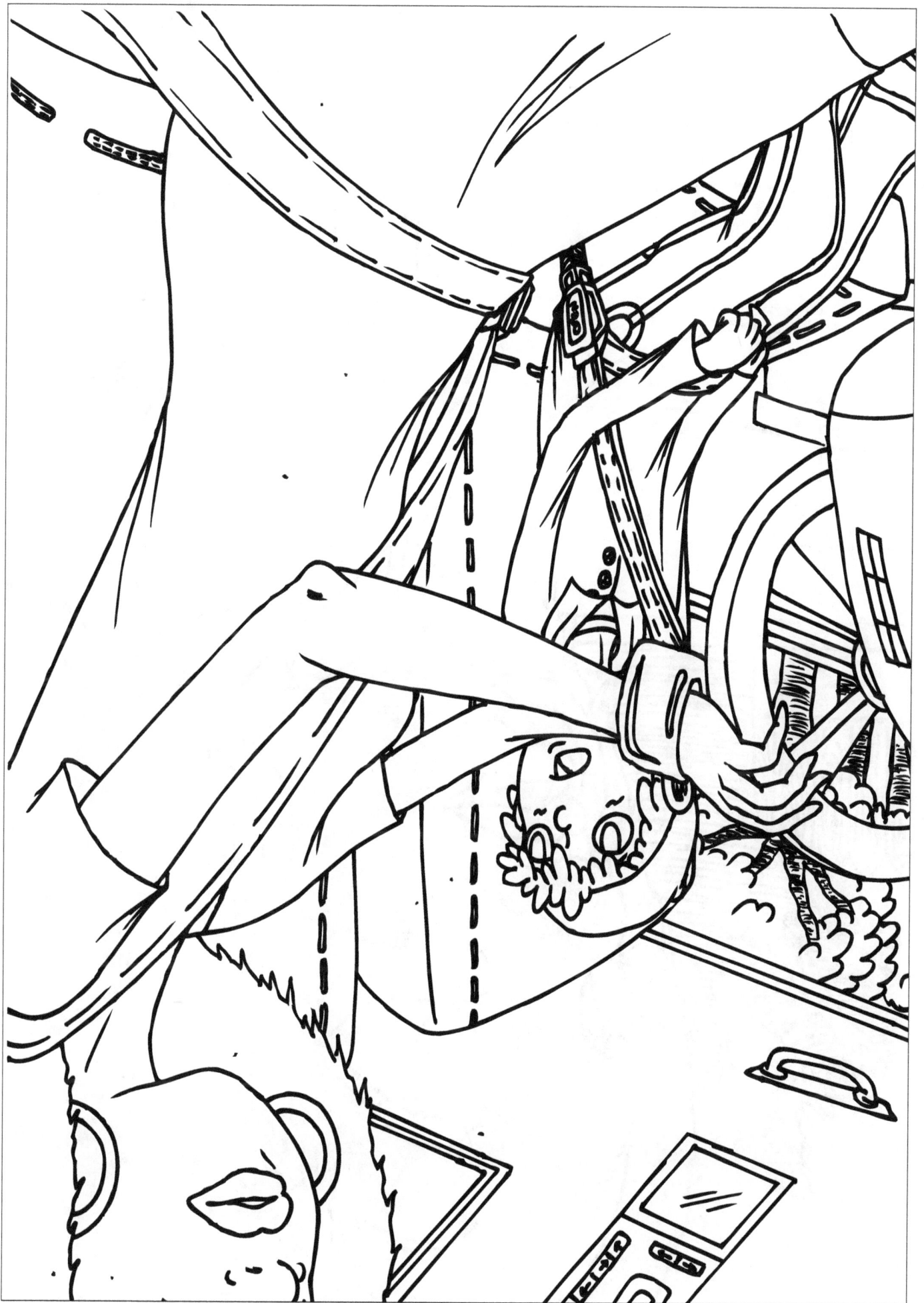

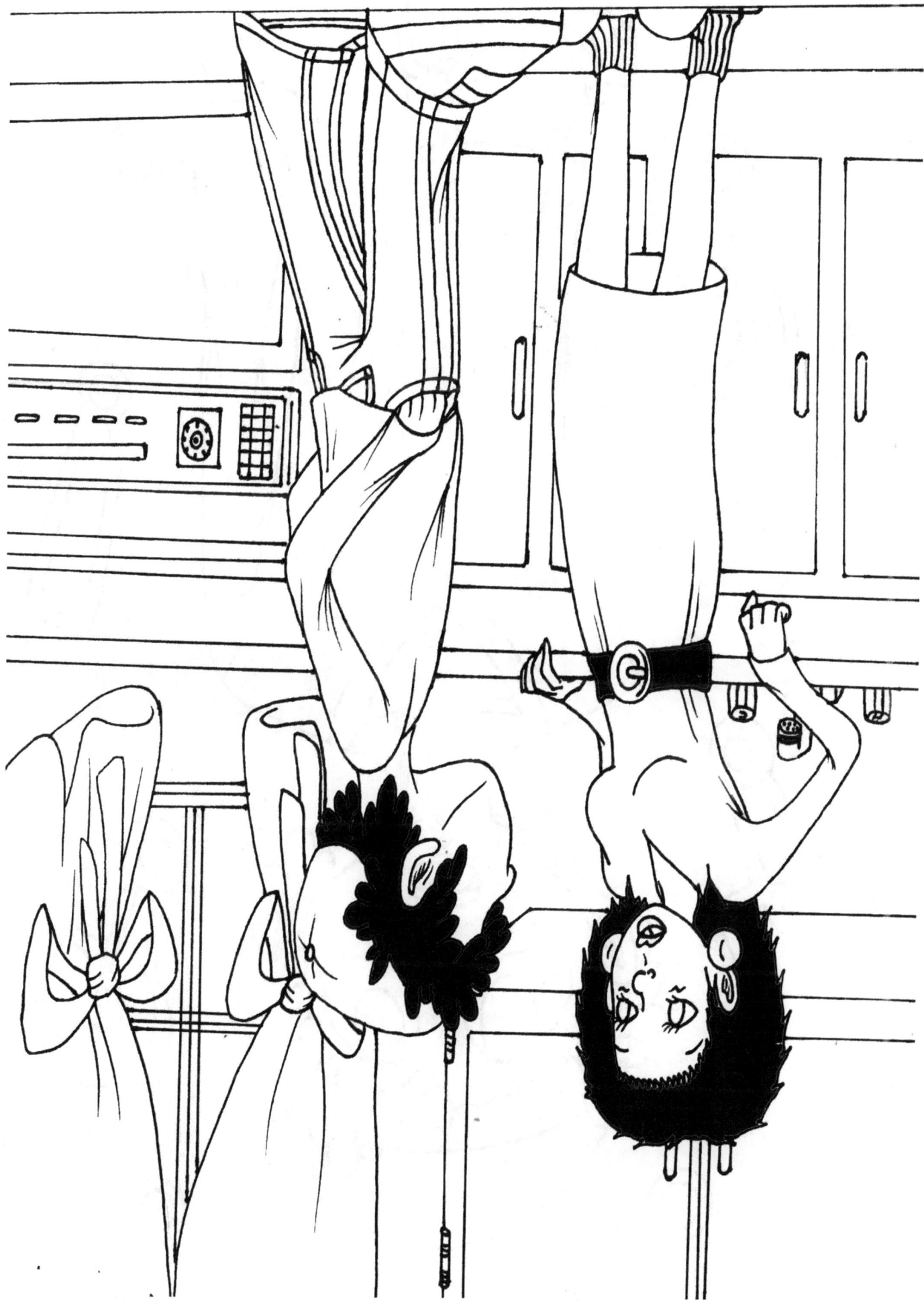

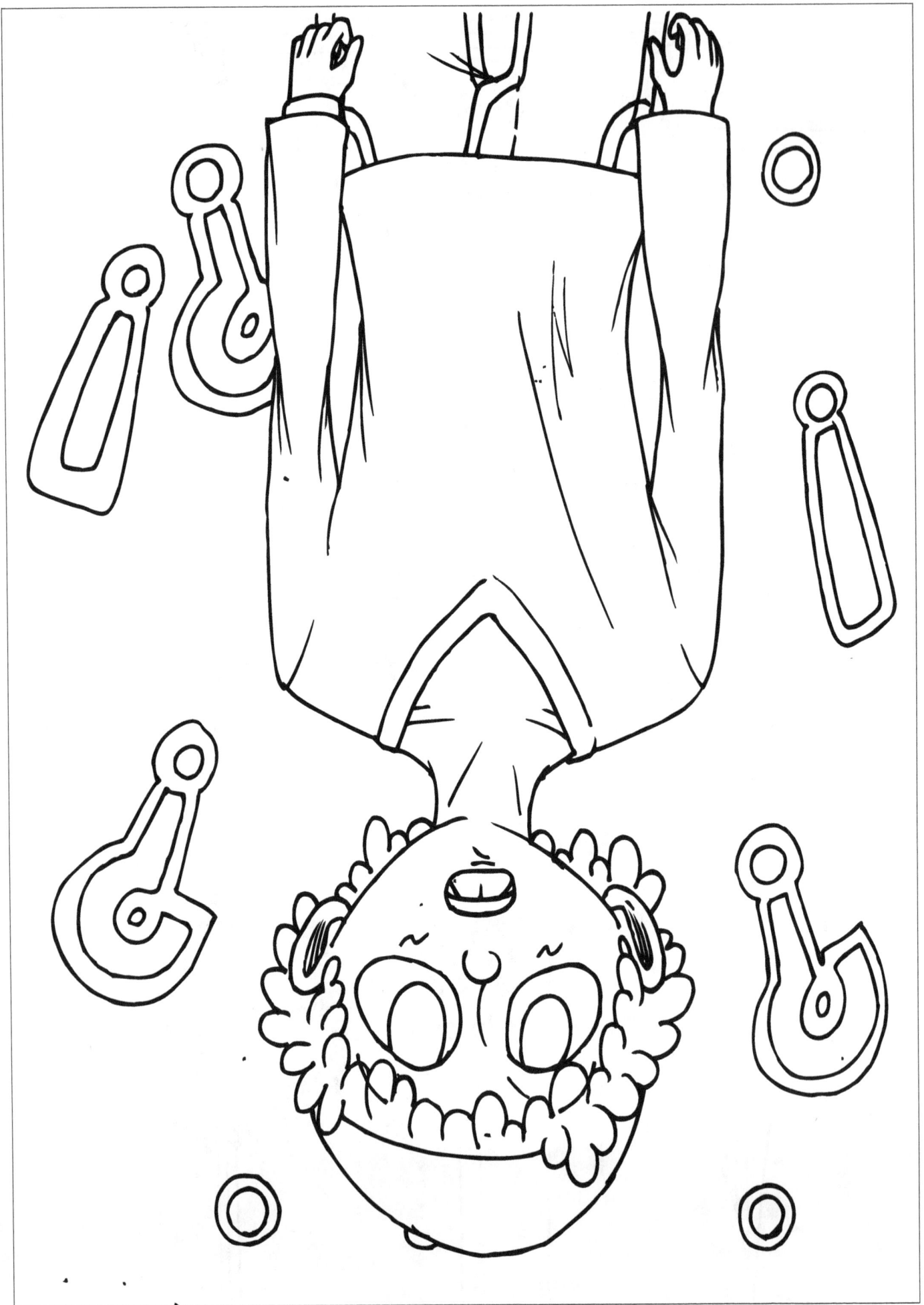

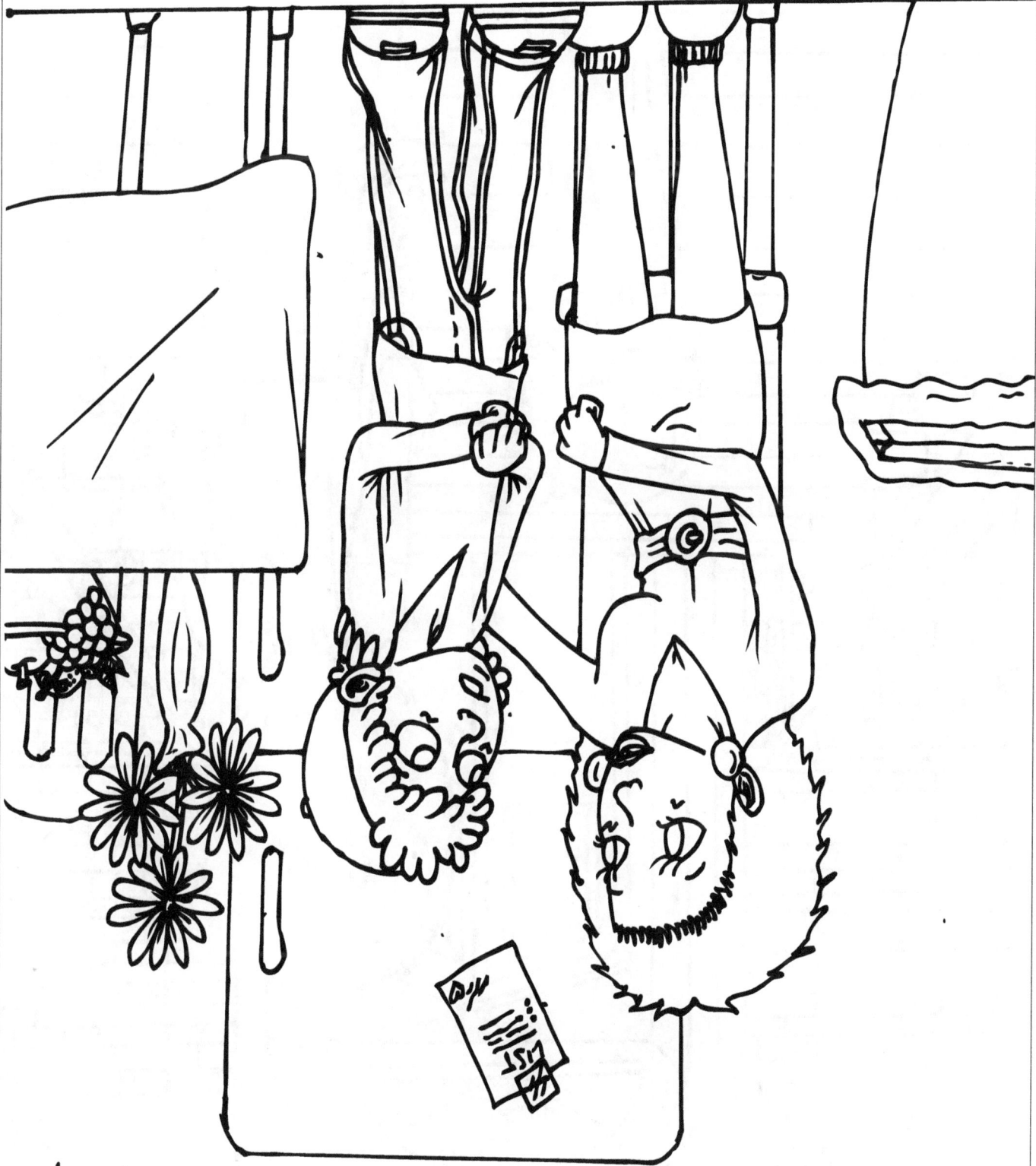

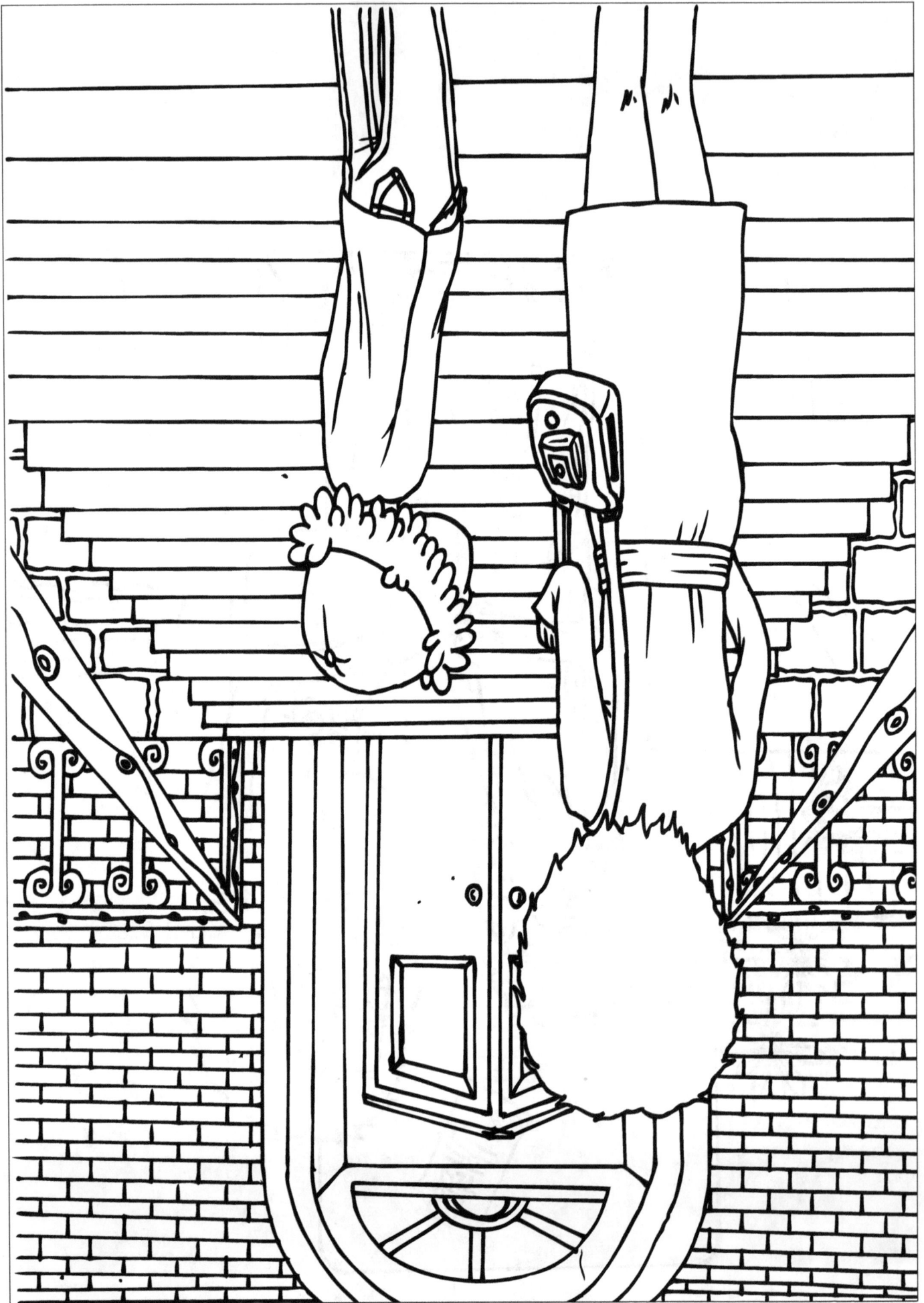

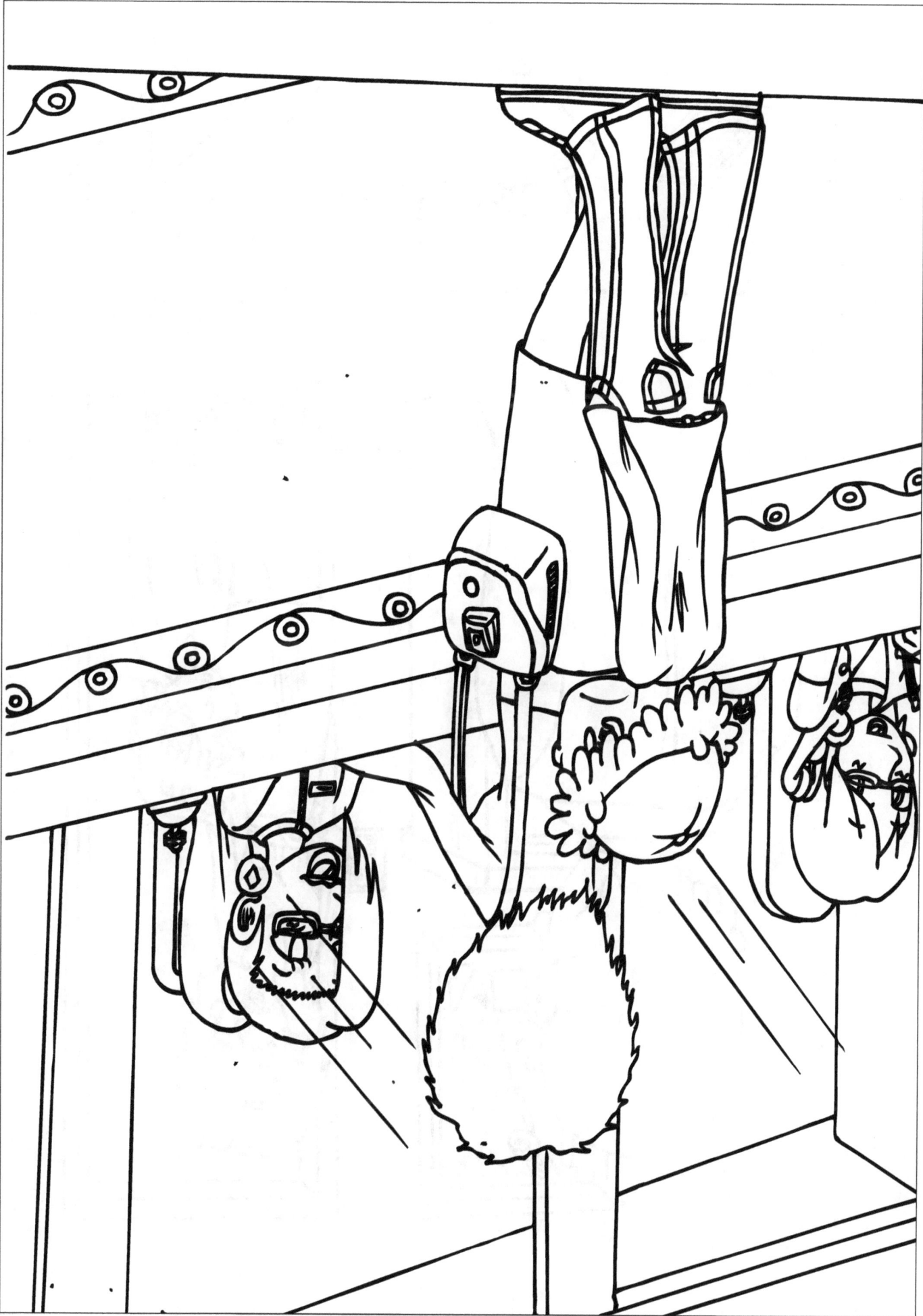

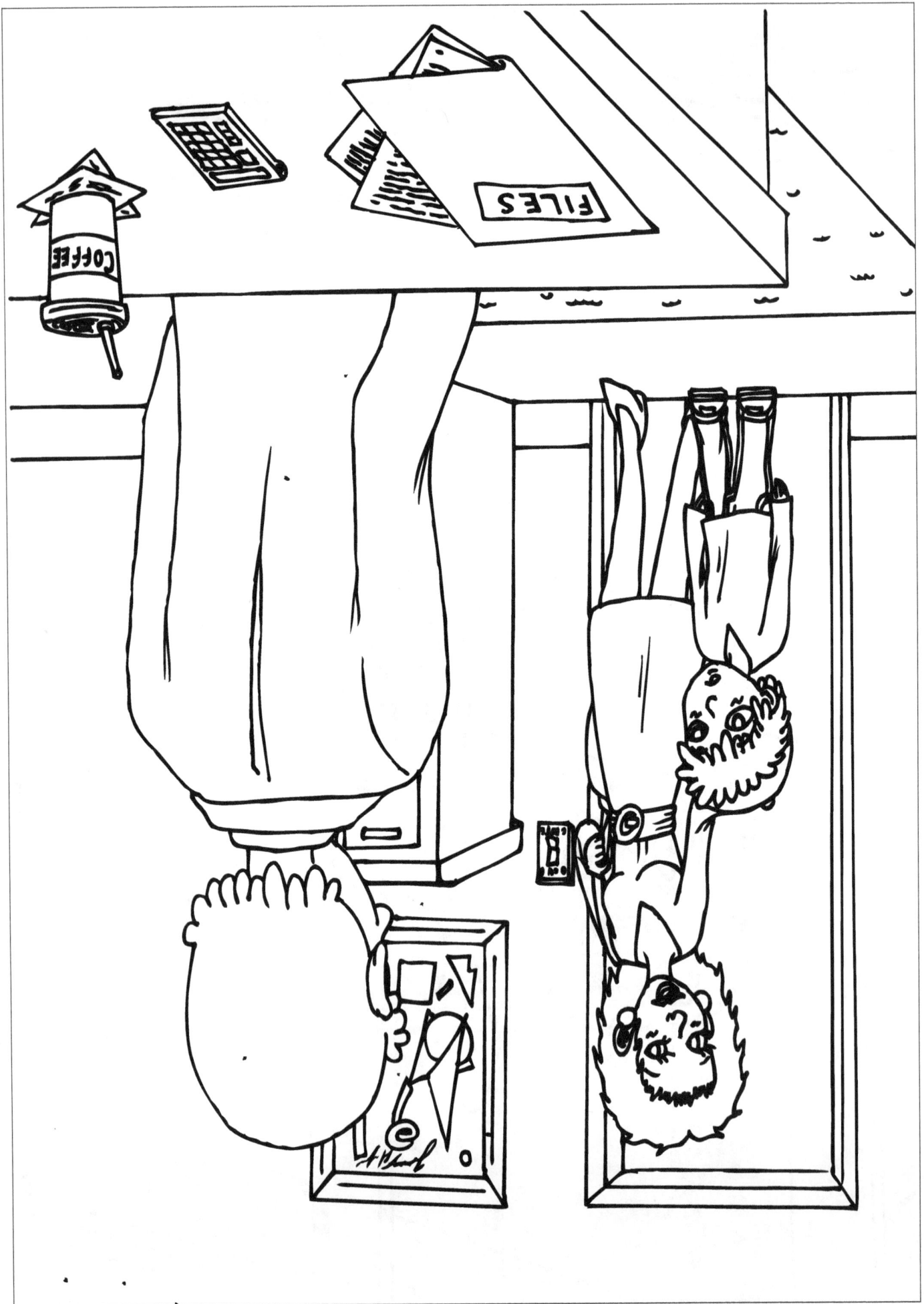

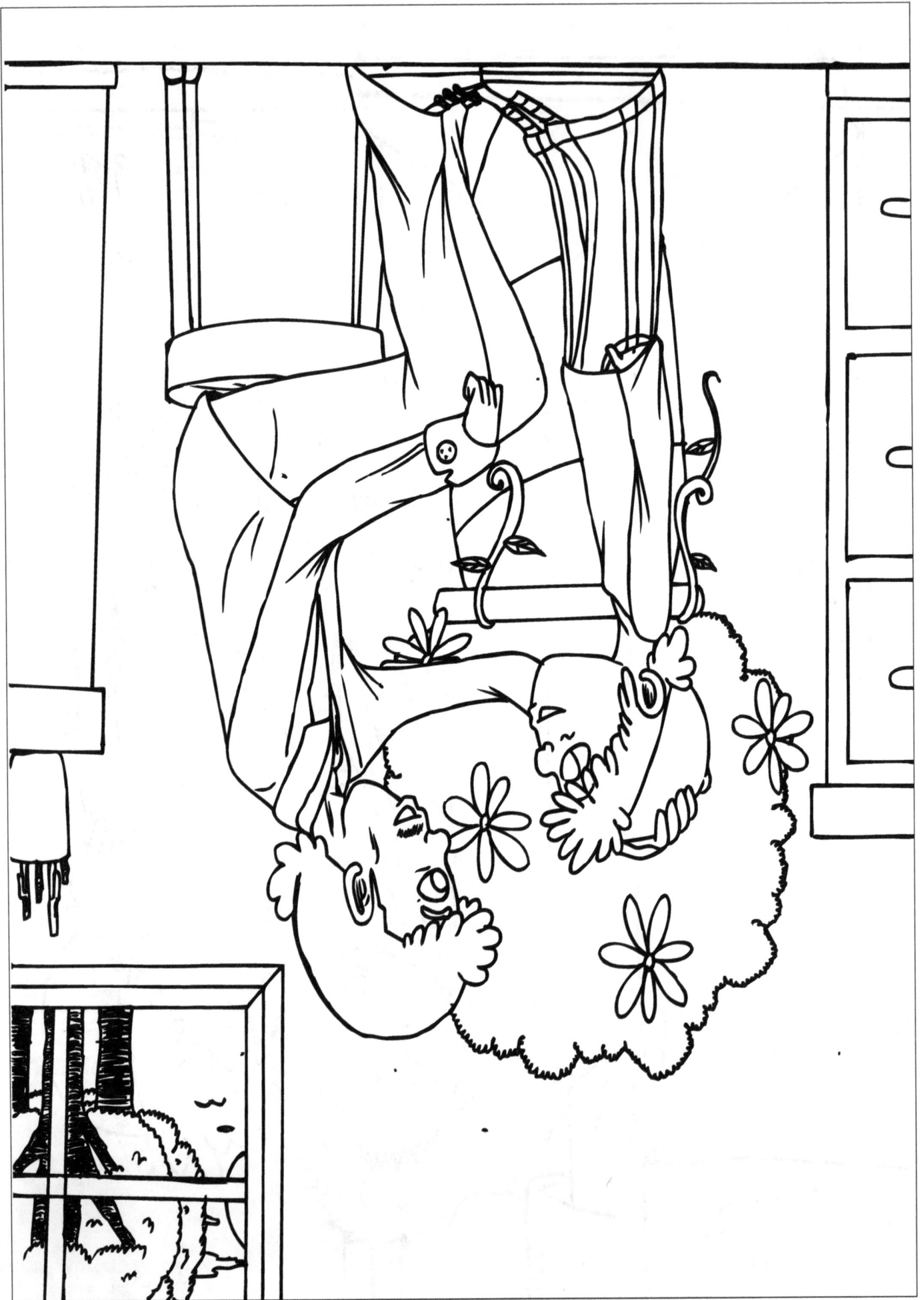

Critical Thinking Questions

How do you think Jr. felt when he realized he was named after his father whom he had never met?

How do you think Jr.'s mom felt when Jr. asked her about his father?

How do you think Jr. felt when he met his father for the first time?

How do you think Jr.'s father felt when he met Jr.?

What do you think will happen next with Jr. and his dad?

Send your suggestions of the ending to the author at info@psmenterprises.com. All submissions will receive a special gift from Mr. Muhammad.

Other Books by Patrick S. Muhammad:
Little Librarian Girl
Wear My Shoes Please!
Mom, Where's My Dad?
Confessions of a 1st Year Principal
From Ordinary to EXTRAOrdinary Author
www.patricksmuhammad.com

Title: Little Librarian Girl
Category: Education/ Charactor Education/ Self Esteem
Distributor: RATHSI Publishing, LLC.
Publisher: RATHSI Publishing, LLC
Paperback: 32pg
List Price: $14.95
PSM Enterprises
(516) 209-3241
www.psmenterprises.com
info@psmenterprises.com

SELF- ESTEEM

Some children give up on their dreams when the odds appear to be stacked against them. Not Patia- Monea, the little girl who wouldn't give up and never stopped until her goals were reached. Learn from the heart touching inspirational children's book that strikes the core of character education.

Title: Wear My Shoes, Please
Category: Bullying/ Charactor Education/ Self Esteem
Distributor: RATHSI Publishing, LLC.
Publisher: RATHSI Publishing, LLC
Paperback: 32pg
List Price: $14.95
PSM Enterprises
(516) 209-3241
www.psmenterprises.com
info@psmenterprises.com

BULLYING

The only way to beat a bully is to face a bully, and that's what three siblings do in this anti-bullying story. Children will gain a better understanding of the value of education and taking advantage of the opportunities that are provided by attaining an education. Even the bully has a wake up call to the importance of school.

Title: Mom, where's my dad?
Category: Family/ Charactor Education/ Self Esteem
Distributor: RATHSI Publishing, LLC.
Publisher: RATHSI Publishing, LLC
Paperback: 16pg
List Price: $14.95
PSM Enterprises
(516) 209-3241
www.psmenterprises.com
info@psmenterprises.com

RELATIONSHIPS

A masterful segway into a difficult question many children are faced to ask today.
Journey through the lens of a young man who finds out the meaning of his nickname during lunch with a friend. From there many unanswered questions unfold. A must have book for school counseling departments.

Title: Confessions of a 1st Year Principal
Category: Leadership/ Administration
Distributor: RATHSI Publishing, LLC.
Publisher: RATHSI Publishing, LLC
Hardback: 145pg
List Price: $24.95
PSM Enterprises
(516) 209-3241
www.psmenterprises.com
info@psmenterprises.com

LEADERSHIP

The Principalship is a position of influence, authority, and heavy responsibility. Colleges and universities provide aspiring leaders with the theoretical framework for the role. However, there is no better training than the day to day training of those currently in the trenches of Principalship. This book is a must have for all school leaders of today. This book will serve as the co-pilot as leaders fly their schools to new heights with a leader educating from the inside out.

About Patrick S. Muhammad

Born and raised in East St. Louis, IL, Patrick was raised to fear only GOD. The youngest of three siblings who all excelled in academics and sports, Patrick used his athletic talents to land a basketball scholarship to Kentucky State University. Upon completion of his bachelor's degree, Patrick relocated to Atlanta to pursue advanced degrees.

While in Atlanta, Patrick began working in the local public school system while simultaneously expanding his entrepreneurship ventures. He has served as a teacher, assistant principal, and principal. Addtionally, he has excelled with several business ventures and found his nitch in the publishing industry.

Patrick is married to Ishtar Muhammad and the proud father of one daughter, Ishlah, and two sons, Ishijah and Ishstafah. They currently reside outside of Atlanta, GA.

PSM ENTERPRISES

Educating From The Inside Out

info@psmenterprises.com   www.psmenterprises.com